a.

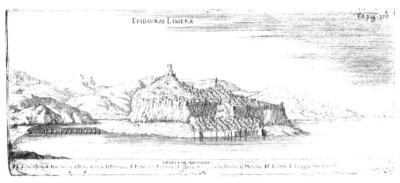

b.

a. Symbol of Monemvasia's prosperity in a copperplate engraving by Coronelli

b. The fortress-city of Monemvasia by Lasor, 1713

NEKTARIOS MILT. MASTOROPOULOS

MONEMVASIA

heir to ancient Sparta,
the invincible city-state of the Middle Ages,
a stronghold of Christianity and Byzantium

Includes a tour of the fortress – city of Monemvasia
followed by a foot journey through the wider area:
**The Vatika – the valley of Asopos
and Molaoi – the highlands of Zarakas**

Natural and historical surroundings, local products

MONEMVASIA 2018

Copyrights

Copyrights ® 2018. Nektarios Mastoropoulos,
Monemvasia, Laconia, Greece 23070
tel: 6980111647 | email: ne.mastoropoulos@gmail.com

Translation: Efrosini Kritikos
email: efrosinikritikos@otenet.gr

Books are not transferable. All Rights Are Reserved.
No part of this book may be used or reproduced in any
manner without written permission, except in the case
of brief quotations embodied in critical articles and
reviews. The unauthorized reproduction or distribution
of this copyrighted work Is illegal. No part of this book
may be scanned, uploaded or distributed via the Internet
or any other means, electronic or print, without the
publisher's permission.

Published In the E.U., Greece, 2018

ISBN: 9781726780278

Aerial photo of the rock by Alexis Stellakis

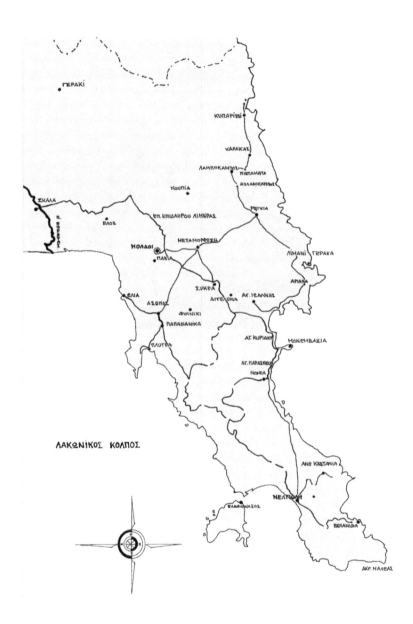

The environs of Monemvasia on a map of the peninsula of Cape Malea

Honorary illustration of Monemvasia inserted on a map of the Peloponnese in the book The present state of the Morea by Randolph Bernard, 1689

Dedicated to my wife
and children

Foreword

"Geologically, Thera is composed of pumice stone and porcelain ..." (Pausanias, 2nd c. AD).

The above extract from the Guide to Greece from which G. Seferis quotes at the beginning of his poem, "Santorini - The Naked Child", kept running through my mind years ago. It was then that I decided to give an answer in relation to the creation and history of Monemvasia. In particular, what are its special features and the very essence of its existence throughout the centuries?

My desire to answer the above questions led me to write this book on the city where I was born and whose unique course makes it exceptional in the history of the Greek nation.

I present this brief historical guide with love and respect. At the same time I embrace the wider area with strolls to unique sites whose millennia long history and unparalleled nature make them worthy of being global destinations and models of sustainable tourism: Monemvasia, the Vatika, the valley of Asopos and Molaoi and the highlands of Zarakas. It is hoped that they are the very first ones to appreciate the unique heritage of their homeland. It is this heritage that we owe today to manage in the best possible manner and of which first, of course, we need to get to know.

Nektarios Mastoropoulos
Monemvasia, 2018

CHAPTERS

PART ONE _____ 1

THE CITY'S HISTORY _____ 1

   1. 2nd century AD. The ages following classical antiquity, Sparta, the invincible city-state still has not lost its glory. _____ 2

   2. 365 and 375 AD. The great earthquake, the tsunami, the destruction and change of the geomorphology of the region _____ 3

   3. Climatic change in the 6th century AD contributes to the decline of Byzantium, the ascent of the Arabs and the descent of the Slavs ____ 4

   4. Fallmerayer, the Slavs and Monemvasia, the theory of the discontinuity of the Hellenic race _____ 5

   5. The Spartans, and in particular those of the 'nobility', settle on the rock of Monemvasia at the end of the 6th century AD. _____ 6

   6. Unique and significant moments in the history of Monemvasia ____ 6

   7. Monemvasia, an impenetrable fortress _____ 9

   8. Andronikos II Palaiologos, 'the godly king' as he is called in various sources _____ 10

   9. Ecclesiastical Privileges _____ 11

   10. Monemvasia is the wealthiest city in the whole empire _____ 12

   11. Its wine: 'monemvasios oinos' or simply 'monovasia' _____ 12

   12. Monemvasiotis from Monemvasia? _____ 13

   13. Two Monemvasiotes play a central role in the events of Constantinople before its fall in 1453. _____ 14

   14. Monemvasia under Papal protection in 1460 _____ 15

   15. The Venetians, rulers of Monemvasia until 1540 _____ 17

   16. The first Ottoman rule (1540 – 1690) _____ 18

   17. The Venetians are once again rulers of the sought-after fortress (1690 -1715) _____ 22

   18. The second Ottoman rule (1715-1821) and the city's great fall ___ 25

   19. Monemvasia during the revolution of 1821, Independence Day on 23 July _____ 26

   20. Yiannis Ritsos is born in Monemvasia in 1909 _____ 29

   21. The Monemvasia of suffering _____ 30

   22. Monemvasia after 1950 _____ 31

PART TWO _____ 37

CHRISTIAN MONEMVASIA THE CHURCHES – THE SAINTS – ITS BISHOPS 37

Saints of Monemvasia, Archbishops and other eminent figures of the city _____ 43
Bishops and other prominent figures of the city _____ 49

PART THREE _____ 55

THE ENVIRONS OF MONEMVASIA. _____ 55
a. The area of Epidavros Limiras _____ 57
b. The monuments of the highlands of Zarakas _____ 58
c. The valleys of Molaoi and the underwater city of ancient Asopos Molaoi, the seat of the municipality of Monemvasia _____ 61
d. The region of the Vatika with its island Elafonisos and Cape Malea Neapoli – Ancient Voion – The Vatika: _____ 62
Pavlopetri across from Elafonisos, the oldest underwater city in the world _____ 63
e. The exclusive beaches of the municipality of Monemvasia _____ 65

LOCAL PRODUCTS _____ 67
1. Viticulture, PDO (protected designation of origin) –Malvasia _____ 67
2. Olive Cultivation _____ 68
3. Products from the past to the present day _____ 69
4. Crop cultivation of the 20th century. _____ 71
Restoration of an old 17th century manor house and grand estate at Agios Stefanos of Monemvasia and the creation of one of the best hotels in the world. _____ 71

PART ONE

THE CITY'S HISTORY

The rock in Locatelli's book by the geographer Coronelli

1. 2nd century AD. The ages following classical antiquity, Sparta, the invincible city-state still has not lost its glory.

Pausanias, the Greek traveler and geographer, visited Sparta in the middle of the 2nd century AD. As he wandered though the city he described only the most worthy of all monuments: 63 sites of worship (sacred shrines and temples); 7 wooden statues; 22 burial sites of eminent citizens; 20 war monuments; 2 colonnades; 24 statues of gods, heroes and Olympic champions; 7 altars; 6 public buildings; 2 gymnasiums; 1 fountain and a multitude of other sites such as Choros, Hellinion and Platanista.

Lithograph print of the rock by D'Aulaire, designed by Baccuet

Copperplate engraving of Monemvasia in the book La sagra lega contro la potenza ottomana

Sparta still retained to a certain degree the glory of its magnificent past, its customs, functions and traditions. At the same time, the coastal cities of the League of Free Laconians had grown significantly. They now cooperated among themselves and functioned independently of its oppressive rule.

2. 365 and 375 AD. The great earthquake, the tsunami, the destruction and change of the geomorphology of the region

These natural phenomena shaped the geomorphology of the region as witnessed up to the present day. In particular, the rock of Monemvasia was created which up until then was not populated apart from the "Minoa", a small observatory on the rocky promontory. According to Pausanias, it was cut off from the mainland and became an islet right off the coast which was later inhabited. The academician, I.M. Panagiotopoulos refers to this rare event as "one of singularity and peculiarity in cosmogony, of the most spectacular ...".

At the same time, the fjord of Gerakas, one of a kind in all of Greece, was created and which would serve as a safe port in the following years to come. Also, some coastal cities were submerged under the sea, such as the city of Asopos and the ancient city of Pavlopetri opposite Elafonisos which is considered today to be the oldest underwater city in the world.

Finally, Elafonisos became an island as the piece of land that connected it to the mainland gradually began to sink. In antiquity it was a peninsula connected to the coast of the Vatika (known as Voies) which Pausanias while visiting the area called Onou Gnathos which means 'donkey's jawbone'. If we take a look at Elafonisos today from a high point in the Vatika, we will instantly understand why Pausanias named it so.

3. Climatic change in the 6th century AD contributes to the decline of Byzantium, the ascent of the Arabs and the descent of the Slavs

A study on the climatic change in the 6th century AD was published in the scientific journal, Nature Geoscience, by a group of scientists in the international interdisciplinary program PAGES, (Past Global Changes) with dendroclimatologist, Ulf Büntgen, as the head of the Swiss Federal Research Institute.

Climatic change during this period is mainly attributed to a series of huge volcanic eruptions which happened consecutively during the years of 536, 540 and 547 AD. The mass accumulation of particles in the atmosphere blocked the sun's rays, which along with a solar minimum, dropped temperatures for decades at about four degrees Celsius. For all these reasons, the researchers in the study claim that it was the most dramatic drop in temperature in the northern hemisphere in the past twenty centuries.

Due to the decline in temperature, there was mass migration of populations from the north to the south of Europe. It was the age when Slavic tribes invaded Greek territory reaching all the way down to the southern Peloponnese. This is one of the reasons why the inhabitants of Sparta abandoned the city for the first time and settled on the rock of Monemvasia, as it is documented in The Chronicle of Monemvasia.

Also, the increase in rainfall in the southern hemisphere led to a more temperate climate which in turn supported an increase in cultivation and food security but also the spread of the new religion of Mohammed.

4. *Fallmerayer, the Slavs and Monemvasia, the theory of the discontinuity of the Hellenic race*

The great question raised in the 1830's with the theories of Fallmerayer, with regard to the actual origins of present day Greeks and in particular those of the Morea, (the present day Peloponnese) is still being discussed today. Fallmerayer claimed that the ancient Hellenic population had been totally replaced by Slavic peoples who had migrated to the area in the Middle Ages, circa 6th century AD.

However, following a controversy that lasted for almost two hundred years, this theory was once again disproved by a study published in March of 2017 in the European Journal of Human Genetics conducted by an international interdisciplinary team of scientists who analyzed the DNA of the present population in the Peloponnese. Findings from the study showed hardly any affinity to Slavic populations since the Slavic settlements in the Middle Ages were limited in number as compared to those of the local native population. It is shown that the Greeks of the Peloponnese have more shared ancestry with other southern European populations and in particular with that of Sicilians and southern Italians and hardly any shared ancestry with Slavic populations therefore finally putting the controversy to rest.

5. The Spartans, and in particular those of the 'nobility', settle on the rock of Monemvasia at the end of the 6th century AD.

The settlement of the Spartans on the rock of Monemvasia must not only have been a sudden movement due to the Slavic raids in the area but most likely was also planned and organized many years before from the age of Justinian in the beginning of the 6th century AD. What is certain is that with the onset of the Slavic raids, Sparta was abandoned and deserted for at least two centuries. However, its glorious history continued on the impregnable rock of Monemvasia, which apart from safety also provided its inhabitants the benefits of its strategic location being in the middle of the Aegean Sea, on the sea routes connecting all four hemispheres.

6. Unique and significant moments in the history of Monemvasia

The Spartan legacy. Monemvasia in essence became the new Sparta, heir to the ancient city, successor of its values, customs and traditions and beneficiary to its privileges. The Monemvasiotes[1] retained their identity throughout the ages as the Bishop of Monemvasia claims in a report to the Patriarch in 1429 AD "την πάτριον και παλαιάν εκείνην των Σπαρτιατών ελευθερίαν τε και ευγένειαν και δώριον αρμονίαν έτι περισώζοντες" (the ancient and ancestral Spartan freedom, nobility and Dorian harmony are still preserved) as quoted in the "Letter to the Patriarch" which was sent by the bishop of Monemvasia in 1429.

As the majority of the first inhabitants of the fortress were Spartans, for centuries the city of Monemvasia was considered the continuity of Sparta and was characterized as the city of the Lacedaemonians and its region as the land of the Laconians, while there are also many references in studies that attribute the name 'Dorida' to it, that is the city of the Dorian Spartans.

Philotheos Kokkinos, the Bishop of Monemvasia from 1341 to 1344, characterized the Monemvasiotes as Dorians in his thesis entitled "The Life of St Isidoros, Patriarch of Contstantinople".

The Monemvasiotes throughout the history of the city, not only did not forget their distant origins of which they felt proud, but also recalled them at every opportunity as in the case when they laid claim to additional privileges or in cases of lawsuits in ecclesiastical or administrative matters.

In addition, all the old documents concerning the entitlements and vested interests of the city were kept under

---

[1] 'Monemvasiotes'(pl. masc.) refers to the inhabitants of Monemvasia, or those originating from the area along with its following forms: 'Monemvasiotis' (sg. masc.), 'Monemvasiotissa'(sg. fem.) 'Monemvasiotisses' (pl. fem.).

special care in the city's treasury vault which is none other than the metropolitan cathedral of Elkomenos Christos.

Self-rule: Even though Monemvasia was under Byzantine rule and was always loyal to the king, in reality, it functioned as an autonomous city-state as its ancestral city Sparta in antiquity.

Monemvasia was ruled by its own elected governor, had its own army and navy and at its height, when the empire was falling, the emperors turned to Monemvasia for economic or military support. Apart from the privileges granted by the emperor such as 'εξκουσσεία', the exemption from military service, first and foremost, they secured their own governmental institutions which they had inherited and upheld from their predecessor, Sparta. As real Spartans they could not have done otherwise.

Its power and wealth.

From an excerpt from the "Letter to the Patriarch" from the Bishop of Monemvasia in 1429 we learn that Monemvasia was wealthy and all-powerful, "θαλασσοκρατήσασα πάσης σχεδόν της εντός Ηρακλείων στηλών θαλάσσης άνωθεν... πολλάς και βαρείας δυνάμεις και στόλους πολυπληθείς Σικελών, Ιταλών, Ισπανών συντρίψασά τε και καταδύσασα πολλάκις." (queen of all the seas above the Pillars of Hercules ... crushed and sank many and weighty forces, multitudes of navies of Sicilians, Italians and Spanish).

The lord of Monemvasia bore the prestigious title of 'Despot' or 'Rex': "Ρηξ δε ην. Ρήγες και γαρ εκ μακρών εν αυτή των χρόνων άρχοντες κεχειροτόνηντο".

Its Privileges: Privileges towards Monemvasia and its citizens were bestowed via decrees, orders, deeds, silver and golden bulls. These documents made up the archive of Monemvasia and were kept at the metropolitan cathedral of Elkomenos Christos. Some of the privileges included powers of self rule, freedoms and laissez-faire policy (tax exemptions).

7. Monemvasia, an impenetrable fortress

Monemvasia was never conquered by force but only through its surrender to hunger following years of siege via sea and land.  Its natural defense due to the impregnable rock on which it is built along with the construction of significant fortifications as well as the morale of its inhabitants, as true descendants of the Spartans, made Monemvasia an invincible fortress throughout the ages. In the Great Chronicle, George Sphrantzes writes in reference to the "υπερνεφελές" (above the clouds) fortress. He says that it is impossible to find on earth, under the light of the sun, another fortress as powerful and invincible and which could put up a resistance to any war machine such as that of Monemvasia.

After his grandfather's and father's failed attempts to capture this 'stubbornly fierce' fortress in 1246, William of Villehardouin subjected the city to an exhausting three year siege, in order to finally manage to occupy it in 1248 after negotiations.

Frankish rule was short lived until 1262 when finally free, Monemvasia experienced incredible growth while at the same time the Monemvasiotes which had left due to the Frankish occupation, founded a second Monemvasia at Pyges, on the banks of the Hellespont in Asia Minor which also enjoyed the privileges of its mother city.

8. Andronikos II Palaiologos, 'the godly king' as he is called in various sources

The Monemvasiotes generously gave their love and devotion to emperor Andronikos who likewise returned it like no other. In his golden bull speech which he gave in 1301, emperor Andronikos expresses his particular care and interest for the city of Monemvasia and its citizens. He praises the city by calling it "περιώνυμον" (celebrated) and describes it as a city which possesses natural fortification and defense and is populated in great numbers. Through his speech we find out that it had wealthy and noble rulers along with advanced industry and a market where surplus abounded. Its residents were able sailors, men of action who were brave and wise.

As the synaxarion of the Virgin Hodegetria, the 'Monemvasiotisa'[2] refers to, Andronikos visited Monemvasia in 1300 and upon his departure all bade him farewell in tears. The emperor deeply touched departed with an oath, saying to them "εγώ θέλω σας πέμψει αντ' εμού Βασιλέα μέγαν και Βασίλισσαν υπερτέρους παντός βασιλέως και αυτοκράτωρος" (I will send you instead of myself a great King and Queen, greater than all of the kings and emperors).

---

[2] In the Orthodox Church, the Synaxarion is an abridged collection of the "Lives of the Saints," read in public worship and in personal prayer.

And truly, after a short while he sent Monemvasia an icon of great value and exceptional art, the Virgin Hodegetria which soon became the protectress of the city known as Our Lady Monemvasiotisa.

As a highlight to his kindness towards the city he gave his famous golden bull speech, an excerpt of which we saw above, where he offers Monemvasia a great number of privileges. The same imperial golden bull is decorated for the first time with an exquisite miniature depicting the emperor offering the same document with the privileges of the city to Christ, that is the Christos Elkomenos of Monemvasia.

"σε διάχρυσο ο Χριστός και στα δεξιά του ο αυτοκράτωρ πατώντας σε πορφυρό μαξιλάρι..."
(Christ in a gold backdrop and on his right the emperor standing on a purple pillow ...).

From Yiannis Ristos' poetry collection entitled "Monovasia".

9. Ecclesiastical Privileges

The bishop of Monemvasia became exarch of the Peloponnese and was from then on called "Παναγιώτατος" (His All-Holiness). He was endowed with the privileges of a Patriarch, while in 1438 the metropolis of Monemvasia was promoted hierarchically to the position of the Patriarch of Jerusalem. This was an important position which was held by its bishop in the Council of Florence-Ferrara which sought ecclesiastical union.

10. Monemvasia is the wealthiest city in the whole empire

Monemvasia during the 13th-15th centuries is not simply a wealthy city but the wealthiest city in the whole empire. Her navy supports Byzantium. The metropolis of Monemvasia provides the greatest of all grants to the Patriarch. In a surviving catalog dated 1324 AD, there is evidence that the annual contribution of the Metropolis of Monemvasia came to 800 hyperpyrons (gold coins) whereas the second largest contribution of the remaining metropoleis was that of Thessaloniki with 200 hyperpyrons.

11. Its wine: 'monemvasios oinos' or simply 'monovasia'

> *"Δωρικόν εκ της Πελοποννήσου Μονεμβασίας"*
> *(Dorikon from Peloponnesian Monemvasia)*
> Nikolaos Houmnos, 14th century

One of the most important products produced in the region of Monemvasia and exported from its port was its famous wine known as **Malvasia** or **Malvoisie** and **Malmsey** in English, thanks to which the city benefited from an enormous amount of incoming wealth.

This was a sweet wine which came from sundried grapes whose vinification methods and practices may have dated all the way back to ancient Sparta and of which were passed down to its descendant Monemvasia as documented in a study by B. Krimbas. He says that the group of Spartans that settled in Monemvasia possibly brought with them to their new home the ancient way of producing wine (fermentation by boiling), similar to Malvazia.

The reputation and quality of the wine was so great that it was not possible to find a noble or wealthy man in all of Europe not to have a bottle of Malvasia wine in their cellar.

Even Shakespeare, in his play "Richard III", makes reference to Malmsey as the means of execution of the Duke of Clarence when he is sentenced to death for treason. When he was granted his last wish he chose to drown in a butt of Malmsey wine!

12. *Monemvasiotis from Monemvasia?*

In those times, the answer to this question was not always obvious.

The activities of the Monemvasiotes and their descendants, due to the privileges given to them by their city, were not restricted to the area of Monemvasia alone. They could also be found at ports throughout the Mediterranean trading and accumulating vast amounts of wealth.

They had a cosmopolitan air about them. They were educated and spoke foreign languages and could be found travelling and associating with the aristocracy in the highest royal courts of Europe.

The term 'Monemvasiotis' had become an honorable title for the descendants of the distinguished families of the city who many times lived far away. However, they never forgot or failed to honor the city of their ancestors of which they were so proud.

13. Two Monemvasiotes play a central role in the events of Constantinople before its fall in 1453.

Two Monemvasiotes led negotiations in Constantinople in 1452 in regards to the unification of the churches. The first was Isidoros of Monemvasia, the papal legate who was working towards unification while the other was Loukas Notaras, the Byzantine Great Duke who was against unification. Even though both were in opposition to each other with regard to religious issues, they both fought bravely on the side of emperor Constantine Palaiologos during the siege and up until the fall of Constantinople on 29 May, 1453.

The renowned **Isidoros of Monemvasia**, now as cardinal and papal legate (the pope's emissary) arrives in Constantinople in 1452 with 200 soldiers in order to reinforce the army with the aim, among other things, to convince the Byzantines of the unification of the churches, something that would ensure assistance from the west. However, this was without any success as the mass held at Agia Sophia for unification did not bring any results and more than anything else led to further division.

He took part in the battles and fought bravely in support of the monarchy and at the last moment evaded death, having disguised himself, and escaped. However, the Ottomans arrested him without knowing who he was and sold him off as a slave and only after dreadful adventures did he manage to return to Rome.

Loukas Notaras was the last Great Duke of Byzantium, who fought bravely during the siege of Constantinople. He came from an eminent family of Monemvasia and had accumulated a great amount of wealth from trade and in particular from salted fish.

He was one of the well-travelled Monemvasiotes who had special privileges along with tax exemptions given to them by their city. His family had settled in Constantinople where they were successful traders.

He was against unification and took part in the negotiations with Isidoros without altering his resolute attitude. Mehmed the Conqueror's historian, Imvrios, attests to the fact that Notaras died dignified and free. He never begged for his life and according to Imvrios the Great Duke was a pious man, devoted to God and who rose above all in wisdom. He was outspoken and had a free spirit. He was valiant, lordly and with spiritual kindness in all his deeds and for this reason he persevered in the positions of the state gaining great political power and wealth.

He initially escaped death and was kept in confinement along with his family. As he was admired for his courage and wisdom initially it appeared that he would have the sultan's favor.

However, the following day the sultan asked for his handsome fourteen year old boy for his harem, which of course Notaras fiercely refused as he knew too well what this would mean for him and his children. He then asked for his children to first be executed before him so as to be sure that they would not be defiled in the harem of the pedophile sultan. Notaras, who had the heart of a lion and the faith of a saint, was one of the greatest martyrs of our nation.

14. Monemvasia under Papal protection in 1460

In 1460 Mehmed II, the conqueror of Constantinople, reached the gates of Monemvasia with his army requesting the surrender of the fortress, the last free enclave in the empire which remained standing after the Ottoman invasion.

Upon the request of the sultan's envoys for their surrender, the Monemvasiotes answered with incredible courage and self-confidence. According to Ritsos they fearlessly responded "we do not rule anything. The Lord on the other hand everything. If it is his wish, he will hand over to you the fortress, houses, belongings and the great key of its entrance."

However, the resilient town could not last for long and for this reason it turned to its powerful protectors. Therefore, delegates from Monemvasia called upon Pope Pius II to take their precious city under his protection.

In this meeting the Monemvasiotes not only remember and make reference to their ancient origins almost one thousand years after the founding of their fortress town but the first thing they say with pride to the Pope is that they are the ancient Spartans.

In his memoirs the Pope writes that the Monemvasiotes had presented themselves to him to ask for their town and for themselves to be placed under his guard. He also stresses the fact that many of them believe they are the ancient Spartans, the power and support of Greece.

The Pope, a luminous figure of the time, was touched when he thought of the ephemeral feats of mankind and wondered how the most powerful city of antiquity with conquests both in the East and in the West, that is ancient Sparta, could now end up weak and begging for its escape from the Ottomans. And thus he took it under his wing.

Pope Pius II placed Monemvasia under his protection in 1461 as he considered the city the successor of Sparta

15. The Venetians, rulers of Monemvasia until 1540

After papal protection, Monemvasia was ruled by the Venetians, the great power of the Mediterranean who at the time were in continual rivalry with the Ottomans. During that time, multitudes of Greeks from other regions ruled by the Ottomans came to the rock of Monemvasia which by then had a population of over 20,000 which was extraordinary for such a small area.

Trade grew as the Venetians undertook projects to develop the city's infrastructure and to fortify its walls They restored the bridge by building it from stone with14 circular arches, a feature which survived until about 1900 when it was given its final form as witnessed to the present day.

16. The first Ottoman rule (1540 – 1690)

By 1537 a new Ottoman-Venetian war had broken out, the third in a row, with the last fortresses of the Peloponnese still under Venetian rule, Nauplion and Monemvasia under heavy attack from the Ottomans. However, they bravely resisted.

Unfortunately, the war did not end well for the Venetians as the Ottoman empire under Sultan Suleiman's rule was at its height. Therefore, after lengthy negotiations, ploys and in the end treason, the Venetians were forced into a demeaning compromise. They were forced not only to pay huge war reparations but also to hand over the strongholds of Nauplion and Monemvasia over to the Ottomans.

In November of 1540 many Monemvasiotes, who had made the bitter decision to leave their town to resettle in other Venetian settlements, gathered at the metropolitan cathedral of Elkomenos Christos. Deeply moved, they took part in holy mass followed by one last litany around the walls of the town holding their holy icons in their hands before boarding the Venetian ships which would take them away forever from their beloved country.

Nevertheless, many inhabitants chose to stay upon hearing the call of the bishop Mitrophan "you good defenders of Christ, stay in your country …". In a moving letter to the Monemvasiotes, which is a ' hymn of love' for the country, bishop Mitrophan urges them to stand up to their enemies on both sides for as he says "it is better to die for your country .. not for the money, not for the glory not for any other reason, but for the ancestral land of our beloved country …".

Under the gaze of Christ and the city's protectress Our Lady Monemvasiotisa at Elkomenos Christos, the town's speechless inhabitants listened to their bishop's circular. In it he says that they would hear the great voice of Elkomenos Christos asking its people where they go. Why do they dare leave his beautiful and god created temple which was once full of words of wisdom and dignity to become a cave of illegal thieves.

However, they did leave taking the priceless icon of Our Lady with them which, unfortunately, was never to be found again. In the years that followed the co-existence of the Ottoman-Turks with the Monemvasiotes who stayed behind voluntarily was overall peaceful in the fortress.

The Ottomans poetically called Monemvasia, Menekşe Kalesi (the castle of flowers), which was still populated and flourishing as trading activity continued from its port which in essence lay in the hands of the Greek inhabitants of the fortress.

Another key event was an episode in the mid 17th century when the fortress was once again attacked by the Venetians. It was by chance that the Turkish guard was far away on a mission and the Monemvasiotes defended the fortress themselves against the Venetians who they obviously did not want as new rulers as they had now become trading rivalries.

It was probably for this reason, as a sign of appreciation, that the Turkish authority of the fortress returned to build the beautiful church of Our Lady Chrisafitissa. It was built circa 1650 in the upper rampart of the town and on which one can discern its Ottoman influences of which characteristic is the church's tower.

In 1668, the Ottoman Turkish scholar Evliya Çelebi visited Monemvasia. He was so impressed that he wrote about the town and its people. We learn that after having travelled 770 miles in the Eyalet of Morea, he found no other such island, so beautiful and so wealthy in goods in all of the Ottoman territory. The people called the fortress of Monemvasia 'Menekşe. The Muslims called it 'Benefshe'. It got its name from its many flowers: violets, daffodils, musk, squill as well as an array of other fragrant flowers. The houses inside the fortress numbered 500 and each one looked like a castle in itself. The settlement was made up of 1600 narrow tile roofed stone houses with many floors and no yard. These houses looked like castles. They were all clean, white and beautiful. In each house there were five to ten cisterns and throughout the whole city 3000 in total. The water which remained in July was considered 'water of life'. A neighbor did not give any away, not even to his neighbor. However, Çelebi speaks highly of the Greeks living in the fortress. He characterizes them as being exceptionally brave and warlike and compares them to seven headed dragons. Çelebi concludes, "God, the creator and provider is the keeper of these fortress-castles [upper and lower city] of the fortress Benefshe ...".

The god-guarded rock by the papal legate Bonaventoura, 1690

Medal which the Venetians distributed in memory of the occupation of the fortress-castle in 1690

PART #1: THE CITY'S HISTORY

Copperplate engraving of Monemvasia by Lykourgos Kogevinas

The city's Lazaretto (quarantine) re- stored by Ioannis Traiforos operates as a hotel today. It was unimaginable dur- ing the medieval ages for such a well- visited city as Monemvasia not to have its own quarantine where goods and visitors were checked and in particular those that came from regions of 'dubi- ous' health standards. The Lazaretto of Monemvasia was built during the sec- ond Venetian rule and in 1710 it had al- ready begun to regulate goods that came from regions which were under control. In a letter dated 1710, Monemvasia is referred to as a capital whose hub is its port.

17. The Venetians are once again rulers of the sought-after fortress (1690 -1715)

In 1669 the Ottomans occupied Crete which was a serious blow to the Venetians who lost their base from which they monitored the seaways of the eastern Mediterranean.

Therefore, they turned to Monemvasia one more time. While the rest of the Peloponnese had already been occupied by the Venetians, Monemvasia was the only fortress in the Peloponnese which was still under Ottoman rule following the lengthy Ottoman-Venetian wars due to the fact that it was invincible.

In the end, Morosini himself, who was now the Doge of Venice, lay a long and heavy siege against Monemvasia by use of an army and navy forcing the Ottomans to finally surrender the city after hardship and hunger in August of 1690.

In this brief period when the Venetians were once again rulers of the fortress, various works to the infrastructure

and restoration of the walls were made which took their final form up to the present day. There were also restorations made to the churches along with the construction of new ones as well as the renovation and construction of new houses. In general significant economic growth is observed in this time.

In addition to all this, the church of Agios Nikolaos was built through a donation by the philosopher and doctor, Andreas Likinios. Unfortunately, the building was never used a church.

A　　　　　　　　　B

Monemvasia was ruled consecutively by the Venetians and Ottomans who showed respect to the world renowned city and contributed to its preservation and prosperity
a. Idealized figure of Venetian authority by Gian-Girolamo Zannichelli
b. Ottoman rule in Historia o sia vero, e distinto raggvagio

18. The second Ottoman rule (1715-1821) and the city's great fall

This marks the worst period of the city of Monemvasia. Once famous and powerful, the city's economic activity was now in decline. Its trade and navy had dangerously decreased along with its Greek element.

To make matters worse, the region underwent total destruction and its population almost disappeared after the Turco-Albanian raids in 1770 as well as the greater part of the southern Peloponnese. It was then, during the Orlov Revolt, when the restless Greeks took part in a rebellion against the Ottoman Turks one more time with the Monemvasiotes along with their bishop playing a leading role. However, once again they were betrayed and subjected to the harsh retaliation of the Turks resulting in the almost total desertion of the wider area of Monemvasia.

Had Monemvasia come to its end?
At the end of this period in 1797, Monemvasia was visited by the French architect Castellan, the early 'photographer' of our area as I would like to call him. This is due to his numerous, realistic drawings almost like photos which he created of our area and the life of its inhabitants.

What would one expect for a traveler to write about the city and its region at its worst state in history following the Orlov Revolt? However, it is impressive if not almost unbelievable that Castellan had pleasant things to say about Monemvasia and its people even in those bleak times:

Those Greeks are the happiest, most charming and active of people. They cross the Mediterranean with their commercial fleets and are the creators, middlemen and tradesmen of the markets of the east. They develop the arts with zeal. They have poets, painters and musicians. And they never forget their ancient splendor. They remember Homer which they read, while the great names of their ancestors make them glow with pride.

The spirit of Monemvasia was still alive. The ties to Ancient Greece had not been broken and their faith was unbending. Their hunger for freedom still ate away at their hearts. Monemvasia's spirit, for whatever that may have meant for Hellenism, had not died.

One can then imagine what the city and its people were like at its height in comparison to what Castellan describes it during the years of its decline.

In contrast though to the above, Castellan does not refer to the Turks in the same flattering way. At one instance he describes his aggravation after one of his explorations of the inner city of Monemvasia where he was initially accompanied by some Turks who had stopped at a spring in the morning and found them at exactly the same place upon his return in the evening without having moved an inch!

19. Monemvasia during the revolution of 1821, Independence Day on 23 July

The time for freedom had come. The mountains of the Peloponnese were full of 'klephts' (brigands) and distinguished Monemvasiotes (such as bishop Chrisanthos, the notable Pangiotakis Kalogeras and Ioannis Despotopoulos), who had been initiated into Filiki Eteria[3], were ready for the great battle.

---

[3] 'Filiki Eteria' or 'Society of Friends' was a secret organization formed in the 19th century in order to overthrow Ottoman rule in Greece in favor of an independent Greek state.

On 22 March, the Ottomans in the area of Monemvasia abandoned their villages and closed themselves in the fortress, while soon after, on 28 March, on the coast opposite the fortress, Greek revolutionary forces from various regions of Laconia arrived. Furthermore, on 3 April the sea blockade of the fortress had begun by a naval squadron which initially consisted of eleven ships from the island of Spetses whose leader was Georgios Panos.

From the beginning of the siege the Ottomans remained unyielding. They stubbornly refused to abandon the fortress as it seemed totally unreasonable to surrender such a 'regal' fortress to what had been their 'slaves' just up until yesterday as I. Filimonas notes.

However, two months after the beginning of the siege, as the food supply had come to its end, hunger set in. They used up all of the rotten millet in storage since the time of Venetian rule. Then they ate all the pack animals that were in the fortress, then all the dogs, cats, rats and any plants that grew on the rock. Of course during the siege they also attempted two times to find food by raiding the nearby villages but without any success. What they found instead were Greeks wide awake and ready to devour them.

In the end, their fierce hunger forced them to surrender the fortress. On 21 July, 1821 its Turkish officers (aghas), signed the protocol for their surrender, handed over the keys to the fortress to Alexandros Katakouzinos and abandoned the city forever to head for Asia Minor.

Naturally, the surrender of the fortress of Monemvasia lifted the spirits of all the Greeks. Ioannis Filimon remarks that the fact that the fortress was finally free was an incredible event that made a great impact on the Greeks.

It was on 23 July, 1821that Alexandros Katakouzinos, head of the liberation forces, entered the gate of the fortress-castle. Along with all the remaining Greeks who had managed to survive the months of attack, the oppression of the Turks and hardship, they all headed towards Elkomenos Christos where they celebrated their emancipation through a moving holy service. Unfortunately, the bishop of Monemvasia, Chrysanthos Pagonis, was not present at the mass, as he had left his last holy breath in the prisons of Tripolitsas where he was imprisoned by the Turks. He was one of the main proponents of the revolution, having prepared the uprising and introduced the divine idea to many.

It was at the midnight mass on the day of liberation that Sior Panagiotakis Kalogeras, the 'archangel' of the city's liberation was present. It was he who risked his life innumerable times, literally walking on a knife's edge while trapped inside the fortress. He did his utmost to help wear down the Turks to surrender the keys of the city to the high commissioner, Katakouzinos.

Also present at the midnight mass was the renowned lady Veneta Koroni, a simple Monemvasiotissa, who turned out to be with her heroism and selflessness, the city's holy figure. Her husband along with two other daring Monemvasiotes swam all the way to the fleet to bring them the message from Kalogeras not to stop the siege but to wait it out because the Ottoman Turks would not last long. The Turks then captured Koroni's wife and tortured her threatening to kill her children so she would confess that it was Kalogeras that motivated her husband and the others in their attempt. She endured the torture and did not betray them and was saved thanks to Kalogera's intervention who had indirectly threatened her captors, making them afraid of their lives when independence came and if any innocent blood was shed by them.

The Turks were terrified and listened to Kalogeras and let go of Mrs Veneta who took her children and left the fortress. As she crossed the bridge she was welcomed as a heroine by the raiders with cheers and gunfire.

> "What torture, Mrs Veneta, to be dragged
> by the hair to the square with your
> three tots by the Vadrouniotes ...".
>
> *Poetry collection "Monovasia" by Yiannis Ristos.*

In the years that followed, Monemvasis was a small, insignificant and isolated village. There was no more reason for anyone to live inside a fortress as it did not offer any added advantage.

However, there was a period (even though the city was not an administrative center) at the end of the 19th to the beginning of the 20th century when there was a cosmopolitan 'air' in Monemvasia, a prominent urban class and some eminent families, among which was the Ristos family.

20. Yiannis Ritsos is born in Monemvasia in 1909

Yiannis Ritsos, the poet, was born in Monemvasia on 1 May, 1909 and later became the most famous of its residents. His father, Eleftherios Ritsos, was a rich landowner in the area and his mother Eleftheria, née Vouzounara, an exceptional figure who introduced her son early to literature and to the arts in general.

However, his father quickly lost his wealth during the years when Yiannis Ritsos along with his sister left for Gytheio in order to go to school there. His mother was also affected by the illness of the time, tuberculosis, and died along with his brother of the same causes.

Ritsos found himself alone and helpless, also suffering from the same infectious disease from which he would suffer for years. The idyllic world in which he lived the first two years of his life fell apart due to death, pain and poverty.

Even though Ritsos lived only twelve years at his birthplace where he finished primary school, he never forgot Monemvasia, the subject of which we encounter throughout his whole poetic works.

It is the subject of suffering and death as he lived it along with his city but also the subject of the fall of the old corrupt world and the struggle of rebuilding a new one in its place, a world of peace, justice and beauty.

21. *The Monemvasia of suffering*

Yiannis Ritsos writes about Monemvasia during this time.

...now there is no one left but a few fishermen and of course the dead ...,

... Tanneries, wineries, textile mills, what silk, what leathers and what fragrant wines, much sought after in the east and the west. There is nothing in this place that betrays the ancient grandeur ...,

... and the work of the rust on the iron fortress gate, in the locks, even in the words of the depth's silence...,

...The only thing left are the bullets on the iron fortress gate, a wide black mosaic with angels, with fishermen, with six-winged glories and way below your name written in bullets as well.

22. Monemvasia after 1950

During that time, at the end of the 1950's beginning of the 1960's, Monemvasia was now a deserted city where very few families lived and where most of the houses were abandoned. Most of its inhabitants had left after the war while at this time the new settlement of Gefyra on the mainland was growing.

One could say that the city's end had come, since apart from everything else, the government had asked from its remaining inhabitants to abandon it as was the case with Mystras and other archaeological sites.

However, the remaining inhabitants of the fortress never abandoned their homes and Monemvasia was never totally deserted while in the beginning of the sixties a new page in its history had just begun.

In the beginning, it was the foreigners and then gradually the Greeks who began to buy the half ruined houses and restore them.

The teacher Mrs. Pitsa Stapa (left) and Mrs. Matoula Ritsou, the owner of the oldest tavern in the fortress-castle (Photo: Antonis Mastoropoulos)

The teacher Mrs. Pitsa Stapa (left) and Mrs. Matoula Ritsou, the owner of the oldest tavern in the fortress-castle (Photo: Antonis Mastoropoulos)

In the meantime the wider area became a tourist destination along with all the advantages that came with this but also some unavoidable consequences.

This is when the couple Kalligas came to Monemvasia, the architects which united their lives with its restoration, a task which they have never abandoned since then. Mrs Haris Kalligas studied like no one else its history which she highlighted in her noteworthy books. The city is greatly indebted to both.

As far as the reconstruction of Monemvasia is concerned, only the restoration of the old buildings was allowed which is still the case today and only after documented study and licensing from the authorities of the Ministry of Culture, which is also responsible for the preservation and restoration of its monuments.

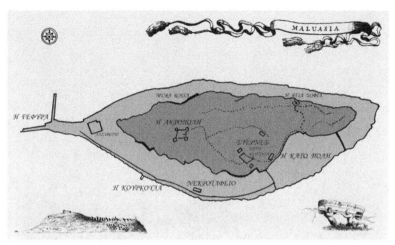

Site map diagrams of the Upper and Lower City in a book by George Koutsogiannopoulos entitled Monemvasia, the queen of the seas

Monemvasia has been officially declared an archaeological site, traditional settlement, historical site and an area of outstanding natural beauty as well as being nominated to be a European World Heritage Site. Monemvasia is an important national asset and its future course should be the main concern of the state in cooperation with the local government and community.

The greater vision of the revival of the Upper Town of the fortress-castle, apart from the necessary investment in its infrastructure along with preservation and restoration, will promote the medieval character of Monemvasia in order to become a world renowned attraction.

Monemvasia's journey, then, through the years, continues

A stroll through the fortress of Monemvasia today.

Crossing the stone bridge over the sea, the only passage to the rock and fortress of Monevmasia, (Monemvasia literally means one entrance), approximately 900 meters away is the gate of the fortress with its old door whose marks from the bullets from the sieges laid to the city throughout the centuries are still visible. Directly above the gate upon entering on the left, a small stone passage leads to a plateau where one can visit the house of the famous poet, Yannis Ritsos, born in Monemvasia in 1909. Intact since Byzantine times, the central cobblestone path of the city is where the commercial district lies, full of shops and traditional cafes and taverns. This path leads to the central square of the city with the canon and museum which once was both a church and a mosque and where one can pay a visit to the city's metropolitan cathedral of Elkomenos Christos.

Following the central path, a small detour on our right leads to the church of Agios Nikolaos. Continuing towards the far south is the other main gate of the fortress-castle which brings us outside the fortress onto a path which leads to the old lighthouse which has been recently restored and well worth a visit.

On our return we reach the southern walls of the fortress where the large square with the beautiful church of Panagia Chrysafitissa lies. A walk through the paths of the city one can admire unique sights characteristic of the medieval town with its old restored houses, monuments and hostels which lead all the way back to square with the canon.

Climbing up to the upper town : from the central square, behind the bell tower is the entrance which leads to the elegant church of the PanagiaMirtidiotissa where the old wood-carved iconostasis which was once placed in the Elkomenos Christos can be seen. Continuing up the path to the upper city, we can admire the rare sights of the byzantine town where the administrators and wealthy citizens of the city used to live.

Upon passing the last houses we follow the path which winds up to the gate of the upper town. As we head on upwards the view of the southern tip of the rocky promontory of Cape Malea in the vast Aegean sea becomes all the more magnificent. On a clear say, we can even see the outlines of the islands of Kythira and Crete to the south and even all the way east to the Cyclades.

Recently, the upper town has undergone major restoration work by the Ministry of Culture. In particular, the complex of the central gate, the byzantine quarters on the left and a little further up the church of Agia Sophia have all been restored. Agia Sophia, built in the 12th century AD, in one of the oldest and most important Byzantine churches in all of Greece. It is stands on the edge of cliff at a height of 200 meters above sea level and is dedicated to

Panagia Hodegetria, which means the Virgin who leads the way. .

In the upper town, we can see huge public cisterns which stored rainwater for consumption throughout the year. Also, well worth visiting is acropolis at the highest point of the fortress which provides a breathtaking view of the whole area which remains unforgettable to all its guests.

PART TWO

CHRISTIAN MONEMVASIA
THE CHURCHES – THE SAINTS – ITS BISHOPS

a b

Christian Monemvasia is not only the churches of the god-guarded city but also all those who served its Church or came from the world renowned city.
a. The Holy Monk Isidoros
b. Loukas Notaras

It must be emphasized that the ancient Greek heritage of Monemvasia was united with its Christian Orthodox faith from its very first moment of establishment. It was the former which they maintained as a legacy and of which its inhabitants were so proud along with the latter to which the Monemvasiotes were always faithfully dedicated.

Up until today, thirty-three churches have been counted in this world renowned site the majority of which were Catholic monasteries and by the mid 15th century occupied about 400 clergymen according to A. Miliarakis. There were also many monasteries, cloisters and churches scattered throughout the interior of the fortress, so many in number that Y. Ritsos calls the commonwealth of Monemvasia the "Holy Metropolis" to be considered the 'Mount Athos of southern Greece' while the same city never ceases to be called "θεόσωστος" (god-saved) and "θεία" (divine).

Of all those churches, many of which lie in ruins, the following stand out:

Elkomenos Christos, the metropolitan cathedral of Monemvasia

The first inhabitants of Monemvasia, having abandoned Sparta along with their bishop Peter, settled in the upper city of the fortress. It is at the site where the holy church of Elkomenos Christos lies today (almost at the center of the lower town) these first inhabitants had built a church at the end of the 6th century.

The history of the city is closely connected with the church on which the years of prosperity and decline respectively have been sketched. In the good years the Monemvasiotes decorated it in many ways, restoring and offering it valuable votives. However, in the hard times such as during the Orlov Revolt in 1770 it had even become a barn and partly destroyed by the Turco-Albanians.

The church was first dedicated to St Anastasia, however, towards the 10th century its initial dedication was forgotten and the worship of Elkomenos Christos began since on its iconostasis[4] there was an icon of exquisite art depicting the Elkomenos Christos under the Cross (that is Christ being driven towards the passion, to the Cross). The icon's beauty was envied by the emperor Isaac II Angelos who secretly stole it to decorate another church in Constantinople.

The second copy of Elkomenos Christos which was put in its place must have been taken with the Monemvasiotes as well as other holy heirlooms in 1540 when they abandoned the town before its Ottoman occupation.

Finally, the third copy which is in the church today is a work dated at the end of the 17th century made in a workshop on Corfu. It is an offering towards the town among the many others of the famous progeny of Monemvasia, the doctor and philosopher, Andreas Likinios, who settled in his ancestor's city during the second Venetian rule which lasted from 1690 to 1715.

Andreas Likinios along with other Monemvasiotes had a tragic end since the Ottoman Turks executed all of them in Constantinople. This was due to his interference in an attempt for the city to not be surrendered to the Ottoman Turks, something which happened in the end anyway, maybe in a deceitful way by the Venetian commanders in 1715.

The church is decorated by another icon of exceptional art, that of the Crucifixion. It is in a special crypt and un-

---

[4] A wall of icons and religious paintings separating the nave from the sanctuary in Orthodox Christian churches.

der the highest security for its preservation and safety as it was recently returned to the town having been found after its theft. The icon, of a Palaiologan style, is a work of art of the 14th century and is one of the most important treasures of our city.

Panagia Chrysafitissa

The church of Panagia Chrysafitissa is the patron saint of Monemvasia today and is celebrated on the Monday after Thomas Sunday following Easter.

According to legend, the icon of the Panagia miraculously disappeared from Chrysafa of Sparta and was found at a site called 'Euresi' next to the church where the only spring of fresh water runs in the fortress-castle.

When some traders from Chrysafa accidentally saw the icon in Monemvasia they thought the Monemvasiotes had stolen it from their village and demanded for it to be returned.

However, the icon miraculously was found again in Monemvasia and since then the worship of the Panagia Chrysafitissa began as she became the patron saint of the city as well as a way to honor the memory of Panagia Monemvasiotissa mentioned above.

The Virgin Hodegetria or St Sophia in the upper town

The Byzantine's Virgin Hodegetria (St Sophia as of 1821), was built in the upper town, on the edge of a cliff in 1150, most probably as a votive offering for thanksgiving for the great victory of the fleet of Monemvasia against the Normans in 1148.

It is the most impressive edifice inside the fortress and on whose south side there used to be a monastery of which only its marble column which supports its tower still stands.

During Venetian rule it was dedicated to Madonna Dell Castello or Madonna Dell Carmino (the Venetians also converted it to a monastery of the order of Cappuccini) while during the first Ottoman rule it was used as a mosque by the Sultan Fethiye or Suleiman.

The church of Panagia Mirtidiotissa (Kritikia)

Saints of Monemvasia, Archbishops and other eminent figures of the city

Peter and John – Theophanes the confessor: Both were worshipped as local saints of Monemvasia for many centuries. Both were particularly active in the restoration of the icons. Peter took part in the ecumenical council of 787 and made several important interventions for the icons and John who succeeded Peter at the metropolis of Monemvasia died persecuted for his faith as a monk under the name of Theophanes.

St Martha of Monemvasia: An excerpt of her life which was written by St Paul of Monemvasia says that St Martha was a nun at the Church of the Assumption of the Holy Virgin Mary of Monemvasia. In the same excerpt there is reference to the miracles she performed in the name of the Virgin Mary. Her memory is honored on 5 May.

St Paul, Bishop of Monemvasia: He was one of the most important clergymen in Monemvasia of the 10th century with a vast education along with his 'soul nurturing narratives' which he wrote and some of which were translated and spread throughout the whole Christian world. He left important information about his times and the fortress-castle.

St Romanos: He was a local saint of Monemvasia who lived in Byzantine times but on whom there is not a lot of information. He is depicted on wall paintings in Monemvasia and in particular in the 12th century byzantine church of Agios Nikolaos.

St Thomas and George of Cape Malea: Saint Thomas led an ascetic life in a monastery which he had built a short distance south of Velanidia in Cape Malea most probably in the 10th century. He is remembered for the very important work he left behind in the wider area. In 1997, under the initiative of His All Holiness Bishop Eustathios, the erection of the Holy Monastery of Androas began and was dedicated to the saint whose feast day is celebrated on 7 July.

St George led a monastic life in the monastery of the same name which he founded between the 13th and 14th centuries at Cape Malea. He was recognized for his education and spirituality and became well known not only in the area but all over the country even in imperial circles which often consulted him. His memory is honored on 4 April.

St Leontios of Monemvasia: Saint Leontios of Monemvasia (whose feast day is on 11 December) was born in 1377 in Monemvasia and for this reason was given the name 'Monemvasiotis'. Saint Leontios was from an aristocratic family. He was the son of Andreas Mamonas, duke of Monemvasia and later commander of the Peloponnese and of Theodora Palaiologina, daughter of the emperor Andronikos IV Palaiologos.

He left Mt. Athos where he led a monastic life circa 1415-1420 and went to Mt. Klokos above the town of Aigio to a site called today, Palaiomonastiro, with its steep cliff where he led an ascetic life.

Later, with the support of his uncles Thomas and Dimitrios Palaiologos he established a magnificent monastery circa 1450.

The admiration of the virtue of St Leontios by the Palaiologos was great and for this reason they donated to his monastery the Passion of Christ, that is part of the Holy Cross, the Crown of Thorns, the Purple Robe, the Rod, the Rope and the Nails which are preserved there intact today.

St Leontios is venerated today with a great church built in his name in the new settlement of Monemvasia in the main town on the mainland called Gefyra.

St Photius of Monemvasia, Bishop of Kievand all of Russia: Photius was born in Monemvasia into a prominent family circa 1377 and received an excellent education. In 1408, at the age of thirty, he was ordained by the ecumenical Patriarch of Constantinople, Bishop of Kiev and all of Russia with a mission among other things to secure the continuous presence of Russia as a member of the Byzantine Commonwealth. In those years he distinguished himself for the reconstruction and development of the Russian church. He has notable writings and in general the Church of Russia is greatly indebted to him since Photius of Monemvasia loved the Russian church and the Russian people for whom he worked with dedication all of his life. He died in 1431 and was buried in the Cathedral of the Dormition in Moscow. His memory is commemorated on 27 May and 2 July.

St Theodore of Kythira, the monk: St Theodore was born in Koroni between 870-890 AD.

When he was of age, he married and had two children. He was ordained a deacon by the bishop of Argos after having seen his many virtues. Theodore later went to Rome on a pilgrimage to the lands of the martyrs. He then returned to Monemvasia where he stayed for many years and was a monk in a cell in the church of Theotokos of Diakonia.

Later he came to Kythira circa 921 AD when the island was deserted and uninhabited due to the raids of the Saracens of Crete and led a monastic life at the Church of the Saints Sergius and Bacchus.

Cristos Elkomenos *Icon of the Crucifixion*

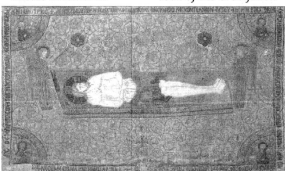

The "Epitaph of Monemvasia", a valuable and exquisite piece of art which is housed in a museum abroad.

This is where he later passed away on 12 May, 922 AD. A short while after his death, sailors passing by Kythira found his relics intact. Three years later in 925 AD some Monemvasiotes who had not forgotten him buried the Saint's relics. The Church of the Saints Sergius and Bacchus was also rebuilt by pious Monemvasiotes and was dedicated to AgiosTheodoros. With the passing of time, a monastery grew there. His memory is honored on 12 May.

St John of Gouves Monemvasia: His life is connected with the tragic events and calamities which took place on our land during the Orlov Revolt in 1770. The ruthless Turco-Albanians who helped the Ottoman Turks to extinguish the revolt in one of their raids in Laconia after having killed Ioannis' father who was a pastor in Agios Ioannis of Gouves Monemvasia. They kidnapped him and his mother and sold them off as slaves. The rage of the Turco-Albanians, especially towards the clergy was great as the bishop Anthimos of Monemvasia had played a leading role in the uprising. Ioannis was barely 15 years old then when he was taken as a slave into a Turkish family in Larisa where he was tortured when he denied to betray his faith and belief in Christ. His memory is celebrated on 21 October.

Agios Ioannis Tourkolekas: (feast day on 16 October) The neomartyr and child martyr Agios Ioannis Tourkolekas was born in the small village of Tourkolekas in Arcadia. His father was Stamatelos Stamatelopoulos-Tourkolekas, a renowned militant of the region of Leontari and his mother Sophia, the sister of the wife of Theodoros Kolokotronis. Among his four brothers, Nikitas stood out as the well-known clan leader known as Nikitaras the Tourkofagos, literally the 'Turk Eater'.

In 1816, Ioannis at the age of 11 at the time along with his father and Anagnostis, the son of the militant of Parnona, Zacharia Barbitsiotis, were arrested and led to Monemvasia where they were executed by the Ottoman authorities as rebels.

They were all beheaded in the yard of the church of Elkomenos Christos in the central square of Monemvasia, first Anagnostis and then the saint's father on 16 October, 1816.

Nikitaras, the saint's brother, bears witness to the martyr's death and to the miraculous sign which god gave. He writes:

They advised my brother to change his faith. They showed him his dead father and told him to let them turn him into a Turk. Then the boy crosses himself and says, 'I will also go where my father goes.' They told him again to become a Turk. But the boy crosses himself once more. His blood became a cross. They took their heads to Tripolitsa.

There, on the marble surface in the yard of the church of Elkomenos Christos the blood of Ioannis formed a cross, the mark of which is still visible today. Their bodies were buried at a site in Monemvasia which still remains unknown today.

The mark of the cross which was formed from Saint Ioannis' blood became a symbol of the struggle for freedom of the enslaved Greeks and a place of pilgrimage.

Bishops and other prominent figures of the city

Important and prominent figures – one could call enlightened spiritual leaders – were the bishops of Monemvasia who played a significant role in the events of the city influencing its course in history and who were the following:

Anonymous bishop of Monemvasia in 1252: Monemvasia persevered as was expected for decades under the pressure of the Latins who as of 1204 had broken up the empire.

This anonymous bishop of Monemvasia fiercely resisted and attempted to prevent the city's surrender in spite of the terrible hardships the city was subjected to. Even after its unavoidable surrender at his own life's risk he never abandoned the city but chose to stay at the side of his flock. The Latins treated him horribly and this holy bishop suffered a martyr's death in Monemvasia due to all the hardship he endured.

Bishop of Monemvasia Nikolaos: Monemvasia is greatly indebted to its seventh bishop, Nikolaos. His education, ethics and activity were contributory factors to Monemvasia's gaining powerful privileges which reached their peak with the golden bull speech in 1300 of emperor Andronikos II Palaiologos. The emperor in his golden bull glorifies the virtues of the bishop of Monemvasia and the inhabitants of the city which is depicted in the seal engraved on the document, offering the Despot Christos (the Elkomenos Christos on the cross) the parchment with the privileges to the metropolis and city of Monemvasia.

Isidore, holy monk, bishop of Russia and finally cardinal of Rome: After the death of Photius, the renowned Isidore was ordained Bishop of Kiev and all of Russia. By coincidence he also came from Monemvasia where he settled in 1407 as a monk and an assistant to the bishop. Isidore was under the protection of the emperor Manuel, who sent him to the Peloponnese after having written the funeral oration which he read himself at the funeral of the despot Theodore I Palaiologos at Mystras, the emperor's brother.

Isidore was performing his duties in Monemvasia at the side of its bishop and this is how he came into contact with the city's archives and came to know all the old documents which concerned its privileges and which were kept in the metropolitan cathedral of Elkomenos Christos. Isidore was also author of the well known "Petition to the Patriarch" in which valuable information about the city of Monemvasia and its history has been recorded.

The letters were in reference to an ecclesiastical battle with the metropolis of Corinth in relation to the diocese of Mani. Isidore along with the bishop of Monemvasia, Kyrillos, travelled to Constantinople to the patriarch to intervene in this matter and won the case. Isidore's education was enormous and multifaceted whereas his life was one great adventure. After the death of Photius of Monemvasia, Isidore was ordanined bishop of Kiev and all of Russia, a position in which he did not prosper since he struggled for the unification of the churches which was something he thought was the only solution for Byzantium to be saved from the Ottomans.

The Russians, however, who did not agree to the unification called him for this reason an 'apostate'. After many adventures he managed to settle in Rome as a cardinal of the Catholic Church. However, Isidore's love and interest for Monenmvasia continued till the end of his life witnessed by the fact that right before his death he bestowed the city with a great gift, that of a great ship.

Bishop of Monemvasia Mitrophan: Mitrophan was bishop of Monemvasia in 1540 which marks a date in history when a new page in history was turned. The Venetians who ruled the fortress at the time surrendered the city to the Ottomans in the autumn of 1540. Many left along with the Venetians whereas there were also many who chose to stay most likely listening to Bishop Mitrophan calling the people to "stay in your country, you righteous defenders of Christ".

Bishop of Monemvasia Hierotheos: He lived in the second half of the 16th century, a very learned man, he was the teacher of Jeremias II of Constantinople. He was always a fearless militant and even risked his life at the forefront of the cause to establish the arbitrariness of the patriarch's fraudulent dismissal from the throne of Constantinople.

Bishop of Monemvasia Dorotheus: He lived and was active during the 17th century and is remembered for his great erudition and writings. His most known work is the Chronicle of Dorotheus which was first printed in 1631 in Venice and was distributed to the whole world and in which valuable historical facts are stored.

Major figures were also:

Theodoros Maurozomes: Lord of Monemvasia when in 1148 with its strong navy the city successfully held out against the Norman raids. This triumpth along with the significant contribution of the bishop of Monemvasia played an important role in the episcopal see to be upgraded to a metropolis. The son of Theodoros, Manuel Maurozomes, almost became the emperor of Byzantium after the Crusaders had left Constantinople.

Nikolaos Eudaimonoioannis: One of the most illustrious and wealthiest men not only of Monemvasia but in the whole empire. He was emperor Manuel's confidante, a very experienced diplomat to whom the emperor gave the most difficult missions. Among other things, he appointed him guardian of his son who was still a minor, Despot Theodore II Palaiologos. Nikolaos always paid tribute to Monemvasia to which he also made many donations and dedications. Among other things, it is well known that he donated to Elkomenos Christos in 1407, the so called "Epitaph of London", a unique piece of artwork, an embroidery of the Epitaph which depicts the dead body of Christ and which is housed today in the London museum. The name of Eudaimonoioannis and the date of his dedication to Elkomenos Christos of Monemvasia is embroidered around the invaluable heirloom which unfortunately does not exist in our town where it belongs.

Panagiotis Nikousios Mamonas: He was born in Fanari, an area in Constantinople in 1613 and belonged to the renowned and powerful family Mamonas of Monemvasia which had moved to Constantinople in 1540. He received an excellent education and spoke five foreign languages and studied among other things mathematics and astronomy. He received a position as an interpreter of the High Porte while later he accompanied the Turkish forces in the occupation of Crete in 1669.

He received generous fees for his services from the Grand Vizier. Due to his position and prestige he would act as an intermediary for his country, Monemvasia but also in general for his nation and Christian Orthodox faith.

Thanks to Panagiotis Mamonas and his tenacious arbitration with Mehmed IV in 1673, the sultan issued a Hatt-i Sharif 5 for various sacred Christian sites also among which were the sacred pilgrimages of the holy lands in Bethlehem and Jerusalem. This was so as those would remain under the jurisdiction of the Greek Orthodox Patriarch, and in this way escaping, at the last minute, the control of the Catholic church which the ambassador of France had attempted to realize on its behalf.

Andreas Likinios: The eminent citizen of Monemvasia, renowned doctor and philosopher, inventor and martyr of Monemvasia who was executed in Constantinople when Monemvasia was occupied for a second time by the Ottomans.

When Andreas Likinios settled in Monemvasia after its occupation by the Venetians in 1690, he built the church of Agios Nikolaos, established a library and donated the third in a row copy of Elkomenos Christos – the holy icon of our city – which we can see today next to the entrance of the church.

PART #2: CHRISTIAN MONEMVASIA

PART THREE

THE ENVIRONS OF MONEMVASIA.

Map of the environs of Monemvasia by Dapper

Many have the impression that when we speak of Monemvasia we mean only the city on top of the rock of the same name.

However, this is not exactly the case since from its founding the wider area was governed and functioned as a whole. It was organized militarily in such a way so as to support the metropolis on top of the rock. To this end, Venetian castles, towers, and other defense structures were built throughout its periphery.

They were all part of a well organized system to monitor all the movements in the area and for the protection of the city where all the inhabitants of the wider area found refuge in times of attack. When the livable space of Monemvasia was limited, as was the case after the fall of Constantinople in 1453, there were serious consequences and its survival was threatened.

Therefore, Monemvasia was in control of the whole area that comprised of almost all of Laconia and reached all the way up to Astros of Arcadia. This historical fact was ignored by the policymakers in the Ministry of Interior in 2010 when the new name of the municipality was proposed to be "Epidavros Limiras". This was the name of the ancient city which was situated a little further north of the fortress of Monemvasia, the name which was given to the whole province in the past.

Then, as mayor of Monemvasia, I played a decisive role to change this proposal. With a unanimous decision of the neighboring municipalities at that time, the name of the greater municipality was finally determined to be "Monemvasia" with its seat in Molaoi.

The present day borders of the municipality of Monemvasia begin from Cape Malea with the last southernmost village of the picturesque Velanidia. They reach all the way up to the border of Arcadia a little further north from the picturesque Kiparissi, covering the whole peninsula of Cape Malea.

This whole area is rich in historical and cultural heritage marked on its landscape in the form of rare and unique sites of environmental interest and great value.

The change in landscape from the coast of Cape Malea (Kavomalia) to the insurmountable Parnon mountains, the diverse geomorphology, the rich bio-diversity, the historical monuments, the local products of high quality and the presence of local tradition in the daily expression of the locals make our area unique.

From all the wonderful things that our region has to offer, we single out some of the best below:

a. The area of Epidavros Limiras

> "the ancient city of old Monemvasia
> Cyriacus of Ancona, 1437

Epidavros Limiras was inhabited a long time ago, in prehistoric times, as Neolithic findings show with obsidian beads which have been found in many caves near this city. Three Mycenaean graves have also been located in the vicinity with numerous pieces of pottery and many valuable grave offerings. These findings show that the city itself had developed into an important Mycenaean center, with agricultural and commercial activity which survived much later after the fall of the Mycenaean civilization in Laconia up until 1100 BC.

According to Pausanias, inhabitants of Epidavros of the Argolid sailing to the island of Kos in order to visit the Ascleipion approached the area in question. Legend has it that a snake that they had brought with them got away and made a hole in the ground where they were to build their new city. Through a dream they had a revelation to settle in this place and build an altar dedicated to the god Asclepius.

They named the city which they immediately founded Epidavros in honor of their metropolis and Limiras which comes from "λιμενήσια" that is a city with a good port.

Some claim that it was named Limiras from the word "λιμός" that is hunger which equates to poverty.

b. The monuments of the highlands of Zarakas

North of Epidavros Limiras there are the highlands of Zarakas which include the port of Gerakas and its ancient fortress-castle, the monastery of Evangelistria and Agios Georgios at Pila of Gerakas as well as Charakas with its Palaiochora and the picturesque Kiparissi.

The port of Gerakas, the "Porto de le Botte" of the Venetians or "Porto Cadena" of Leake, is a natural fjord whose main characteristic is its calm waters and the fact that it is totally hidden from view while travelling on the coastline. It has been inhabited since Dorian times when it was 'the bone of contention' between the two powerful Dorian states, that of Argos and Sparta. Later, during Roman rule the city took part in the League of Free Laconians and went through a quiet time of peace and prosperity.

Impressive is its fortress along with its acropolis which are on the peak of the hill suspended above the port which today may lie in ruins but whose walls where visible can still be seen standing as a witness to its past. They testify to its power, historical course and the safety it provided to the whole coastline since prehistoric times.

The monastery of Evangelistria and Agios Georgios at Pila of Gerakas is situated high up on the rock of Pila opposite the sea. It is reachable by following the path connecting the port of Geraka with Reihea. At about midway lies a side path which leads to Pila and ultimately to the monastery.

The Katholikon[5] of the monastery is a tall, white temple with a unique architectural feature: it has two sanctuaries, one built on top and inside the other.

The lower sanctuary is dedicated to Agios Georgios. However, a very narrow and steep internal staircase on its left end leads you to the sanctuary above dedicated to the Virgin Mary the Evangelistria. Further up within the church's tower there is even another small church dedicated to Agia Paraskevi.

The monastery was built a few years before the middle of the 19th century. Its keeper was the monk Konstantinos Stournaras or Kiriakos, who was highly educated. The monk, leading an ascetic life in a remote cave in the area situated at the site of what is known today as Balogeri, could see a light on the opposite cliff burning every night. He went to the site in search for an answer to this mystery and found the icon of Agios Georgios[6] and on this very site (most likely in place of another Byzantine church,) he built a church with the contribution and help of the devout people of Zarakas, the monastery of Agios Georgios.

Later and for a long time the monastery was abandoned and deserted and came under the jurisdiction of the monastery of Zerbitsis. However, since 1980 under presidential decree the monastery was declared independent and only for women. As a result, today the monastery operates within a significant community of monasteries that have a large spiritual reach.

In the head village of Reichea, with its traditional houses and hospitable inhabitants, one can visit the Folklore Museum of **Reichea** which has some amazing exhibits de-

---

[5] *The major church building of a monastery.*

[6] *"Agios" is the Greek word for "Saint" or "Holy", its feminine form is "Agia".*

picting life in the village hundreds of years ago. A little further down are the crystal clear secluded beaches of Vlihada and Balogeri where you can go spend the day or even camp out at night.

Charakas with its Palaiochora Charakas is a small, quaint and well kept village built amphitheatrically at the foot of the ridge of the mountain Myne at an altitude of 600 meters. It has many charms: its wild landscape, its valley, the traditional stone houses as well as its cleanliness. Apart from its natural beauty, Charakas also has an interesting and rich historical past in which its Palaiochora stands out.

The Palaiochora of Charakas is a Byzantine settlement, abandoned and deserted on the edge of the ravine of the site of Stavros, a short distance from present day Charakas. It was probably built during the Slavic invasion by farmers and shepherds of the Eurotas Valley who found refuge in the ravines, caves and precipices of the Parnon mountains, as well as the valley of Charakas where the Palaiochora was founded.

The picturesque Kiparissi
Kiparissi is situated 10 km north of Charakas, at the inlet which is formed at the point where Chionovouni mountain meets the Mirtoan Sea. It is made up of three large 'neighborhoods': Paralia, Vrisi and Mitropolis.

It is a unique tourist destination, with exceptional beaches, one of a kind sites for climbing, traditional houses and hostels.

c. The valleys of Molaoi and the underwater city of ancient Asopos Molaoi, the seat of the municipality of Monemvasia

The settlement is first recorded in a document in 1209 and specifically in the "Treaty of Sapienza". It is first found with a minor corruption in its name, in the form of 'Mola'. The treaty in question had been drawn up between Geoffrey of Villehardouin, leader of the Franks, and the Venetians who helped the crusaders in the fall of the Byzantine Empire and the occupation of the Morea.

During the Orlov Revolt, Molaoi underwent major destruction by the raids of Turco-Albanian forces. It was liberated at the beginning of the revolution of 1821 but was laid to ruins after the raids of Ibrahim in the area. Upon the liberation of Greece, it became the seat of local government and as of 1864 the capital of the province of Epidavros Limiras.

Even though today is has taken the shape of a modern city, there are many sites that give witness to its deep historical roots. There are graves and notable Mycenaean findings at the site of Gagania as well as mineral wealth at the same site. One can visit the hill of Vigla with the remains of an ancient acropolis on its peak, the old tower, a medieval structure on the rock of Agia Paraskevi as well as Larnaka Gorge which crosses right through the middle of the town.

The gorge, which has its own water source, was where the first settlement was founded and which later in Byzantine times grew into a large economic center.

On the peak of Kourkoula mountain there is also a castle where the locals used to take refuge in the case of attack and from where they kept watch on the whole area all the way up to Monemvasia.

The ancient city of Asopos developed in the region of Plitra during the Classical and Hellenistic period. The city was initially under the influence of Sparta, that is it was one of the cities of the Perioeci. However later, during Roman times, it participated in the common cause of the League of Free Laconians and enjoyed the favor of the Roman emperors under which it experienced great growth and prosperity.

The writings of Pausanias and Strabo, as well as a series of inscriptions and coins, all speak of the admiration they all had of the glorious historic course of the city. However, tectonic forces, as evidence shows, led to its abrupt end, if not to its very existence, certainly to its population and economic growth.

There have been studies on this natural transformation according to which the southern Aegean and Laconian earth due to the rift which divides the lithospheric plate of Europe and Asia with that of Africa, experience many tectonic forces and are subjected to continuous sinking. The rift along the Greek fault encircles the Peloponnese and has caused many changes as the sinking of the mainland at the same time leads to a rise in the sea level. This rise has been estimated at one meter every one thousand years.

d. The region of the Vatika with its island Elafonisos and Cape Malea Neapoli – Ancient Voion – The Vatika:

It is the southernmost city in continental Greece and is situated at the site of the ancient city of Voion.

Voion was an ancient city which was founded between 1050 and 950 BC by Heraclides Voion and which belonged to the League of Free Laconians. The city flourished during Roman times as a trading port but declined in later antiquity. Later, various settlements emerged known as the Vatika (a corruption of the word Voiatika). The present city also known by the name of Neapoli was designed in 1837 by the Bavarian architect Birbach who had also designed the cities of Sparta and Karystos.

Neapoli is connected to Kithira and Antikithira by ship. It has an important archaeological museum and a maritime museum with impressive exhibits from the maritime tradition in the area.

With the new road which connects Monevmasia and Neapoli via Agios Fokas, the distance between the two cities has decreased considerably facilitating transport to and from the area.

Pavlopetri across from Elafonisos, the oldest underwater city in the world
The ancient city of Voion which Pausanias describes in his writings in the 2nd century BC lies a few meters under the surface of the sea a short distance away from the islet. It is believed that it was submerged in 375 BC by the same earthquake that destroyed Gytheio.

According to a study by Dr. Iakovos Stamoulis and Elias Kroupis, the earthquake measured over 7 to 8 on the Richter scale. It was probably even greater since the same event is associated with the formation of Gerakas, Monemvasia, Plitra and even most likely of Kithira. The size of the earthquake contributed to the phenomenon of rapid sand displacement on the sea's bed transforming vast areas of land to a lagoon of quicksand in an instant. This led to the break of the peninsula of Onou Gnathos from the mainland and the creation of present day Elafonisos.

"There is no doubt that this is the oldest underwater city in the world" claimed Dr Jon Henderson, professor of underwater archaeology at Nottingham University in reference to Pavlopetri.

Dr Henderson emphasized that "there have been findings that date from 2800 to 1200 BC, that is far before the glorious days of Classical Greece. There are even older underwater cites in the world, however, they are not considered to be as organized as this city which makes it a unique case."

He goes on to say, "We have found more than 30,000 square feet of buildings which had not been discovered. However, what really surprised us is the discovery of a possible mansion, an impressive and monumental building with a huge rectangular antechamber which makes it probable that this city was inhabited by an elite class which automatically 'upgrades' the status of the findings."

Kastania cave This is a safe cave in the village of Kastania considered to date back three million years ago. It is made up of two levels whose length totals 500 meters. It showcases stalactites and stalagmites of rare beauty and is accessible to the public to visit.

The petrified forest in the wider area of Agios Nikolaos, Voion
This is an enormous geological monument made up of an ancient 'graveyard'of flora (palm trees) but also of shells which thrived in the area millions of years ago. Today it is a testament to the region's geological past, an area of special paleontological importance which make it a unique natural monument worth visiting and experiencing.

The fortress-castle of the Vatika
The fortress-castle of Agia Paraskevi is built on top of rocky heights in the valley of Voion, in the vicinity of the Vatika as is mentioned in the Chronicle of Morea. It is 1.8 km away from Neapoli, near the villages of Mesochori and Faraklo. The site, recently restored by the Ministry of Culture, strategically controls the Laconian bay and the wider mainland.

e. The exclusive beaches of the municipality of Monemvasia

Beaches of the south coast, in the Mirtoan Sea: The beaches on the south coast extend all the way from Monemvasia to Zarakas. They are mostly pebble beaches protected by southern and southwestern winds due to their location.

Beginning from the north, at Kiparissi we will find Agia Kiriaki, Megali Ammo and Drimisko and at Rihea the beach of Vlihada. Near the village of Gerakas is Kochilas and in the area of Agios Ioannis there is Old Monemvasia where you will find Kastraki and the well known Pori which has been awarded with a blue flag.

The crystal clear beach in the new town of Monemvasia is called Kakkavos and has been awarded a blue flag while before the main gate of the fortress there is the protected Kourkoula and under the shade of the fortress rock lies Portelo.

Heading south we come to the exceptional and awarded beaches of Nomia, at Abelakia of Ksifia and Agios Fokas.

Beaches on the west coast of Laconia: Of sand or small pebbles with a view of the mountains of Mani and calm waters, the beaches of the west coast include some of the most interesting attractions for visitors.

Beginning with picturesque Elia where we find Cavo, the small cove at Limani, as well as Viandini and Tigania which has been awarded with a blue flag as we head south towards Asopos. There one can take a swim at Boza and if we want more action we can choose to go to Plitra, the second beach in the area also awarded a blue flag. The beach Charachia with its pebble in a multiple array of colors and the organized beach of Pila can both be found in the village of Daimonia while our unique Archangelos with its golden sand has also been awarded a blue flag.

Beaches of Cape Malea and the Vatika: The beaches of Voion (or the Vatika) and Cape Malea are of impressive diversity. The most northern beach towards the west is the stunning beach of Marathia while at the bay of the Vatika with impressive turquoise waters we will meet the well known beaches of Pounta, Maggano and Nertziona. These three beaches comprise one single fairy tale like sandy beach the length of five kilometers. Even though it is situated right inside the city, the beach of Neapoli is sparkling clean and organized. It is not by chance that it is awarded annually with a blue flag.

Behind the small port of Palaiokastro lies protected, Ammitsa and to the south, Aspes and Rismari. In the unique landscape of Agia Marina lie the hidden beaches of the Petrified Forest. Finally, on the side of the Mirtoan Sea, the beach Panagia is an ideal choice for the visitors of Kastania Cave while at the same time the exceptional beaches of Velanidia will cool off those who manage to reach the magnificent edge of Cape Malea.

Of course, no one should miss the chance to go on an excursion to the heavenly Simo beach on Elafonisos. One of the most famous beaches in Greece.

LOCAL PRODUCTS

1.Viticulture, PDO (protected designation of origin) – Malvasia

The viticultural zone of the PDO wines of Monemvasia-Malvasia was established in 2010.

The zone of the PDO wines of Monemvasia-Malvasia is in the southeastern tip of Laconia in the peninsula of Epidavros Limira which ends at Cape Malea on the outer edge of the present day municipality of Monemvasia . It is required that the wine undergoes oxidative aging in barrels for at least two years.

The wine varieties of **PDO Monemvasia-Malvasia** is monemvasia, at a percentage of 51%, asirtiko, asproudes and kidonitsa. The white variety of monemvasia is cultivated extensively as well on the island of Paros which make up the white and red wines of PDO Paros.

Kidonitsa is a characteristic local variety of Laconia and contributes to a wide variety of wines in the area either on its own or with other white varieties such as a similar variety of wine characteristic in Laconia called petroulianos.

Asproudes is an unidentified family of a white variety which contribute to the wines of PDO Mantineia.

PDO wines of Monemvasia-Malvasia: sweet white

a) from sun-dried grapes (sun-dried, vin liastos/vin de raisin passerile)

b) liqueur wine from sun-dried grapes (liastos, vin de liqueur de raisin passerile)

2. Olive Cultivation

In the 12th century the Byzantines and foreigners considered the Peloponnese and in particular the region of Monemvasia as one of the most important olive producers in the world.

The Frenchman Pouqueville in 1799 in reference to the olive production notes that, "The Morea is probably the area with the most numerous and beautiful olive trees. The cutting of a branch could be considered a crime … . The earth everywhere in harmony with the climate demand the cultivation of the olive tree …".

After the unsuccessful Orlov Revolt our region paid a high price. Its valleys were set on fire by the Turco-Albanian forces who for ten whole years ravaged the area.

The onslaught of Ibrahim in 1825 completed the destruction. He set up his base in Molaoi on 5 September, 1825 from where he led his assaults burning the area to ashes.

Nevertheless, many olive trees have been saved which are over one thousand years old. It would be a shame if it was our generation which allowed for this valuable treasure to be lost.

3. Products from the past to the present day

Malvasia Wine: The cultivation of Malvasia wine began before the 13th century in the wider area of Monemvasia and spread to other areas throughout the whole world. It was renowned in the markets of the East and West. Today, the wine Malvasia in the region of Monemvasia has gained protected designation of origin (PDO) status due to its historical origins and past which have remained unaltered throughout the centuries.

Oil: Its production increased significantly with its introduction by the Venetians and soon became to be one of the main exports not only as an edible product but also as raw material for soap manufacturing.

Silk and Dyes: Silk and dyes such as imperial purple 'porphyra' were produced in Monemvasia for export to the West.

Flax: It was cultivated throughout Laconia and the Peloponnese. Thread made from the stem of flax fiber was used to make ropes and sacks among other things.

Dried figs: In the past, there was mass production of dried figs in Laconia and Messenia. The figs were strung and dried on a rope and then exported. About two million pieces were made according to the topographer, William Martin Leake (1806).

Onions: They were exported from Monemvasia and most likely from the area of the Vatika as well as throughout the Peloponnese. Today the cultivation of the renowned Vatika onion still continues. It is hoped that it will be given the status of protected designation of origin soon.

Wheat, maize and millet: Today's plains full of olive trees were once treeless and were sowed with seeds to feed the local population with staple foods as well as to stock the storage houses of the fortress-castle.

Leather and hides: A large part of exports came from Laconia where stockbreeding was highly developed and in particular goats and sheep. Many tanneries operated next to the fortresses.

Honey and wax: Munster, in his cosmography in 1550, makes reference to the fact that Monemvasia is known for its wine and honey. The rare and rich flora of the area has contributed to the production of exceptional quality honey since ancient times.

4. Crop cultivation of the 20th century.

At the beginning of the 20th century there was extensive fig cultivation. After 1970 the olive became the main crop to be cultivated resulting in the area becoming a huge olive grove. In the wider region there is still cultivation of citrus fruit, vegetables, pomegranate, carob, prickly pears and herbs to mention but a few.

Local olives.

The local olive variety, athinoelia, has been in the region of Monemvasia for thousands of years and to which the old olive trees in the area give testimony.

Restoration of an old 17th century manor house and grand estate at Agios Stefanos of Monemvasia and the creation of one of the best hotels in the world.

The manor was built in the 17th century near a spring whose flowing water gave life to the surrounding fertile lands. The spring water was stored in a cistern on the estate which gave the manor its name in the form of "Kinsterna". Kinsterna comes from the Ancient Greek κίστη (kístē) which means box that later became the Latin cisterna (water reservoir). It was reborrowed into Greek during Byzan- tine times as kinsterna which survives today as a testament to the long history of the estate.

Still visible today are the Ottoman features of the building such as the small defensive openings, the large chimneys, enigmatic inscriptions and the great fire- places all intermingling with Byzantine and Venetian elements such as mosaics, ceramics and marble designs.

As the Ottoman era came to its end, its local landlord, Ibrahim Bey, handed it over to the prominent families Ristos and Kapitsini. The last 'Lady' of Monemvasia, Lina Kapitsini, lived in the manor up until the late 1970's before she passed away leaving the property to its own fate.

The restoration of a gem

In 2006, Antonis Sgardelis, a native to the area and the new owner of the manor, began its restoration along with a group of architects, engineers and designers with the use of traditional methods and local building materials. In 2010 Kin- sterna was resurrected into a five star boutique hotel including its enormous estate of olive and citrus groves, vineyards and vegetable gardens which are harvested by its very own guests. Its old wood oven has been restored and now makes fresh bread served daily at its restaurant along with organic produce straight from its gardens. Guests can enjoy its signature wine and 'tsipouro' a brandy made from the remains of grape after pressing for juice from the old wine press brought back to life. Its very own olive oil is produced using ancient crushing methods with large stone mills turned by donkeys which are bred on its land along with the many other animals such as sheep and horses.

Today, apart from being one of the best hotels of its kind in the world, Kinsterna is a model of ecological sustainability. At the heart of its identity lie the values and beliefs that have shaped its cultural heritage and are now being kept alive through the preservation and revival of biodiversity, cultural landscape and traditional knowledge systems that have been handed down for generations.

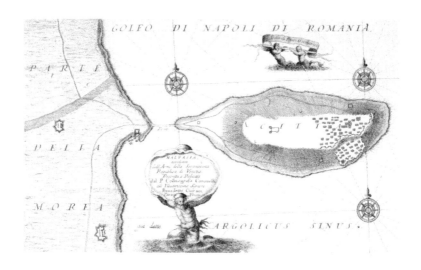

Top view of the rock of Monemvasia by Coronelli

Wood-engraving of the rock from a drawing by H. Belle

Top view of the rock from Locatelli's book Racconto historico della Veneta

Watercolor painting of the rock by G. Piperopoulos

Details of the Lower City by Kon. Malea

The 'godly' king Andronikos offers the golden bull to Christ, miniature from the golden bull

Flag used by Pierros Tzanetakis during the siege of the fortress in 1821

The siege of the fortress in 1821 by Alex Isaia

Turkish aghas hand over the keys to the fortress to Alexandros Kantakouzinos by P.V. Hess

Distinctive corners in the fortress-castle of Monemvasia (Photos: Antonis Mastoropoulos)

Distinctive corners in the fortress-castle of Monemvasia (Photos: Antonis Mastoropoulos)

The church of Agia Sophia or the Virgin Hodegetria in the Upper City

The church of Agios Dimitrios and Antonios

House in the Lower City (Photo by Antonis Mastoropoulos)

The central square with the canon and museum (Photo by Antonis Mastoropoulos)

Aerial photo of the rock a. by Alexis Stellakis b. by Antonis Aronis

Aerial photo of the rock a. by Alexis Stellakis b. by Antonis Aronis

a. View of the fortress-castle of Monemvasia from the walls of Epidavros Limiras, a drawing by Castellun

b. The church of Evangelistria and Agios Georgios in Gerakas

c. Aerial photo of the lagoon of Geraka by AntonisAronis

Watercolor paintings of houses at the port of Plitra by G. Piperopoulos

Ruins of the ancient city of Asopos at the site of Kokkines in Plitra

View of the valleys of Molaoi in a watercolor painting by G. Piperopoulos

View of the valleys of Molaoi from the foot of Mt. Kourkoula

| Wrcolor painting of the ruins of a watermill at the Gorge of Larnaka by G. Piperopoulos | View of the Old Tower of Molaoi and the ruins of the aforementioned watermill |

Detail from a mosaic floor in the first Christian church at the site of Chalasmata in Molaoi

Aerial photos of Neapoli and the island of Elafonisos by Antonis Aronis

Nektarios Mastoropoulos: Who I am?

I was born in 1966 in Monemvasia where I was raised and have lived almost all of my life. I studied mathematics at the University of Crete in Heracleion.

I have been married since 1991 with Argiro Mavraki, a teacher from Chania, Crete and we have two children, Adamantia and Miltiades.

I have worked in education both in the private sector and in the public school system. At present I am teaching at the high school of Monemvasia and before this I worked for the Center for Environmental Education in Molaoi, Laconia.

I have been a representative in the local government for twenty years and have been elected mayor of Monemvasia three times.

In my free time, I study local history and occupy myself recreationally with organic farming. I am interested in local sustainable development: local products, health, diet and nutrition, the preservation of traditional seed varieties and the conservation of Greek domestic animal breeds.

Made in the USA
Coppell, TX
26 March 2022

75604917R00057